Obento

Snack Pack 2

おべんとう

Sue Xouris

NELSON
CENGAGE Learning™
Australia • Brazil • Japan • Korea • Mexico • Singapore • Spain • United Kingdom • United States

Obento Snack Pack 2
1st Edition
Sue Xouris

Editors: Yoshi Abe, Rani Kellock, Craig Metcher
Publishing editor: Margherita Ghezzi
Senior designer: Vonda Pestana
Text designs: Vonda Pestana, Yuri Tanabe
Text illustrators: U-Suke, Ami Sharpe
Cover designer: Vonda Pestana
Photo research: Corrina Tauschke
Production controller: Hanako Smith
Reprint: Jess Lovell
Typeset in Kyokashotai and Gill Sans by Yuri Tanabe

Acknowledgements
The author would like to thank the following for their invaluable, assistance, advice and support:

Kyoko Kusumoto, Japanese language consultant
Yoshi Oguro, for language advice
Takeshi, Kimiko and Shun Takahashi
Osamu and Mutsuko Takahashi
Satoru, Kyoko and Chiyumi Tsuchiya
Takuo and Satsuki Tsuchiya
Tokyo Gakugei Daigaku Fuzoku Koganei Primary School, Mr Kawabata and class 5C
Koki, Fumiko and Sato and their families
Yue Tanabe
Tomoyasu, Akihiro and Hiroki Taguchi, Takumi Yagi
Akiko Kobayashi and the Kobayashi Family
Saki Atobe, Natsuki Yamaguchi, Hideya Takayanagi and Megumi Chiba from Nirasaki High School
Shaunagh Compton, Caitlin Connelan, Emily-Bryce Dowle and Jack Colwell and Year 8 students from Cronulla High School
Arryn Terman, Jenna Lincoln, Samuel Barguana and Kyle Davis from Kirawee High School
Avril Burt
David Hines
Kate Xouris, for many song ideas and the name Snack Pack
Milly Xouris, for the voiceovers
Nick, Kate, Ben and Milly Xouris for their unwavering support.

For product information and technology assistance,
in Australia call **1300 790 853**;
in New Zealand call **0800 449 725**

For permission to use material from this text or product, please email
aust.permissions@cengage.com

National Library of Australia Cataloguing-in-Publication Data
Xouris, Sue
Obento Snack Pack 2

For secondary school age
ISBN 978 0 17 013546 7

Japanese Language - Textbooks.

495.682421

Cengage Learning Australia
Level 7, 80 Dorcas Street
South Melbourne, Victoria Australia 3205

Cengage Learning New Zealand
Unit 4B Rosedale Office Park
331 Rosedale Road, Albany, North Shore 0632, NZ

For learning solutions, visit **cengage.com.au**

Printed in Australia by Ligare Pty Limited.
5 6 7 8 9 10 11 16 15 14 13 12

Contents

indicates you need the teacher's CD-ROM to complete this task

suggests you to check out the Internet for more information and resources

indicates your teacher has extra material for you to complete this task

indicates this is a game to play in class [the teacher may have extra instructions and worksheets]

①いちばんすきなこと

All my favourites!

Here in Book 2 it's your chance to talk about the things that interest you and find out what interests your friends and family. It's all about what you love and what you hate. And the topics ... well, that's up to you! You'll find the categories in the buttons around the edge of the page and you and your teacher can choose which ones you want to learn more about. First, you learn the pattern and then you can talk about whatever you like!

The SNACK Buttons!

Food たべもの (ta be mo no) for more, go to page 8

People's Houses うちで (u chi de) for more, go to page 36

At School がっこうで (ga k ko u de) for more, go to page 38

Movies えいが (e i ga) for more, go to page 30

Drinks のみもの (no mi mo no) for more, go to page 12

Games ゲーム (ge e mu) for more, go to page 40

Japanese Food わしょく (wa sho ku) for more, go to page 42

Eating Out レストランで (re su to ra n de) for more, go to page 44

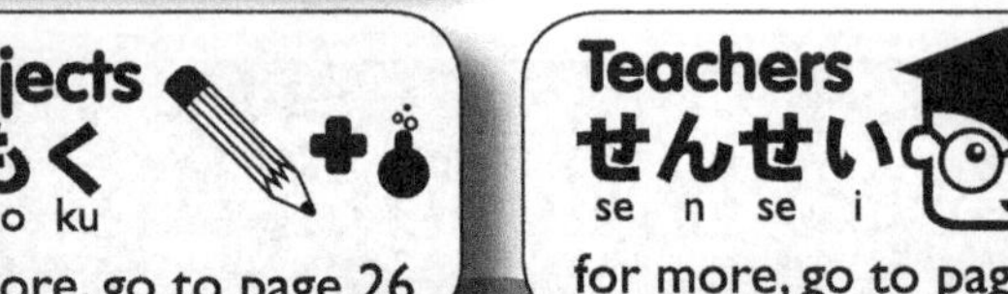

TV Shows テレビばんぐみ (te re bi ba n gu mi) for more, go to page 30

Daily Life せいかつ (se i ka tsu) for more, go to page 34

The big questions

Use these expression and the snack buttons to practise with your friend asking about likes and dislikes. All you have to do is put a "snack" (sport, food,...) in the blank space!!

You can simply give your answer (even in English if you like!) followed by the word です (*desu*).

What ______ do you like?

すきな ______ は なん です か。
su ki na ______ wa na n de su ka

What ______ do you not like?

きらいな ______ は なん です か。
ki ra i na ______ wa na n de su ka

Pop over to the CD-ROM and have a close look at the patterns with your teacher then come back and **choose your snack!**

CD ROM

NEW STUFF きょうのポイント

Now, what do you love? And what do you hate?

Here's your chance to talk about all of those things you like and also all of those things you don't like.

The pattern is simple and all you have to do is put the category like sport or food or animal in the [ ] and the thing which is your favourite like tennis or chocolate or elephant in the ( ).

Have a close look at the pattern and practise it with your teacher. Use the snack buttons to help you.

すきな [ ] は ( ) です。
su ki na wa de su

The [ ] I like is ( ).

きらいな [ ] は ( ) です。
ki ra i na wa de su

The [ ] I don't like is ( ).

What do you like THE MOST?

Don't forget! You can put いちばん (*ichiban*) on the front of the sentence to make it the one that you like or hate THE MOST.

E.g. いちばん すきな たべもの は すし です。
i chi ba n su ki na ta be mo no wa su shi de su
My most favourite food is sushi.

Meet Professor Porgy.
He is the inventor of the Porgy Colour Code Grid Capacitor.

It works like this:

Colour the top row purple
Colour the left column orange
Colour the は (wa) red
Colour all of the other boxes green
Colour the です (desu) yellow

Fill in the blank boxes yourself.
You can then put your sentences together using the PORGY colour code, that is: you must always follow the Purple-Orange-Red-Green-Yellow order!!

P	O	R	G	Y
1st purple すきな su ki na	2nd orange たべもの ta be mo no	3rd red は wa	4th green チョコレート cho ko re e to	5th yellow です。 de su

You can't go wrong!

Use the grid to make up some sentences with your partner. Remember to follow the P-O-R-G-Y code!

PURPLE / ORANGE	すきな su ki na like	きらいな ki ra i na dislike	いちばんすきな i chi ba n su ki na most favourite	いちばんきらいな i chi ba n ki ra i na most hated
たべもの ta be mo no FOOD	チョコレート cho ko re e to chocolate	さかな sa ka na fish	アイスクリーム a i su ku ri i mu icecream	ピザ pi za pizza
のみもの no mi mo no DRINK	ジュース ju u su fruit juice	コーラ ko o ra cola	ミルクセーキ mi ru ku se e ki milkshake	コーヒー ko o hi i coffee
スポーツ su po o tsu SPORT	バスケットボール ba su ke t to bo o ru basketball	ラグビー ra gu bi i rugby	テニス te ni su tennis	ゴルフ go ru fu golf
いろ i ro COLOUR	あか a ka red	ピンク pi n ku pink	あお a o blue	オレンジ o re n ji orange
どうぶつ do u bu tsu ANIMAL	いぬ i nu dog	ねこ ne ko cat	コアラ ko a ra koala	へび he bi snake
かもく ka mo ku SUBJECT	かがく ka ga ku science	ちり chi ri geography	にほんご ni ho n go Japanese	すうがく su u ga ku maths
せんせい se n se i TEACHER				
テレビばんぐみ te re bi ba n gu mi TV SHOW				
えいが e i ga MOVIE				
タレント ta re n to CELEBRITY				
ゲーム ge e mu GAME				

RED は wa	YELLOW です de su

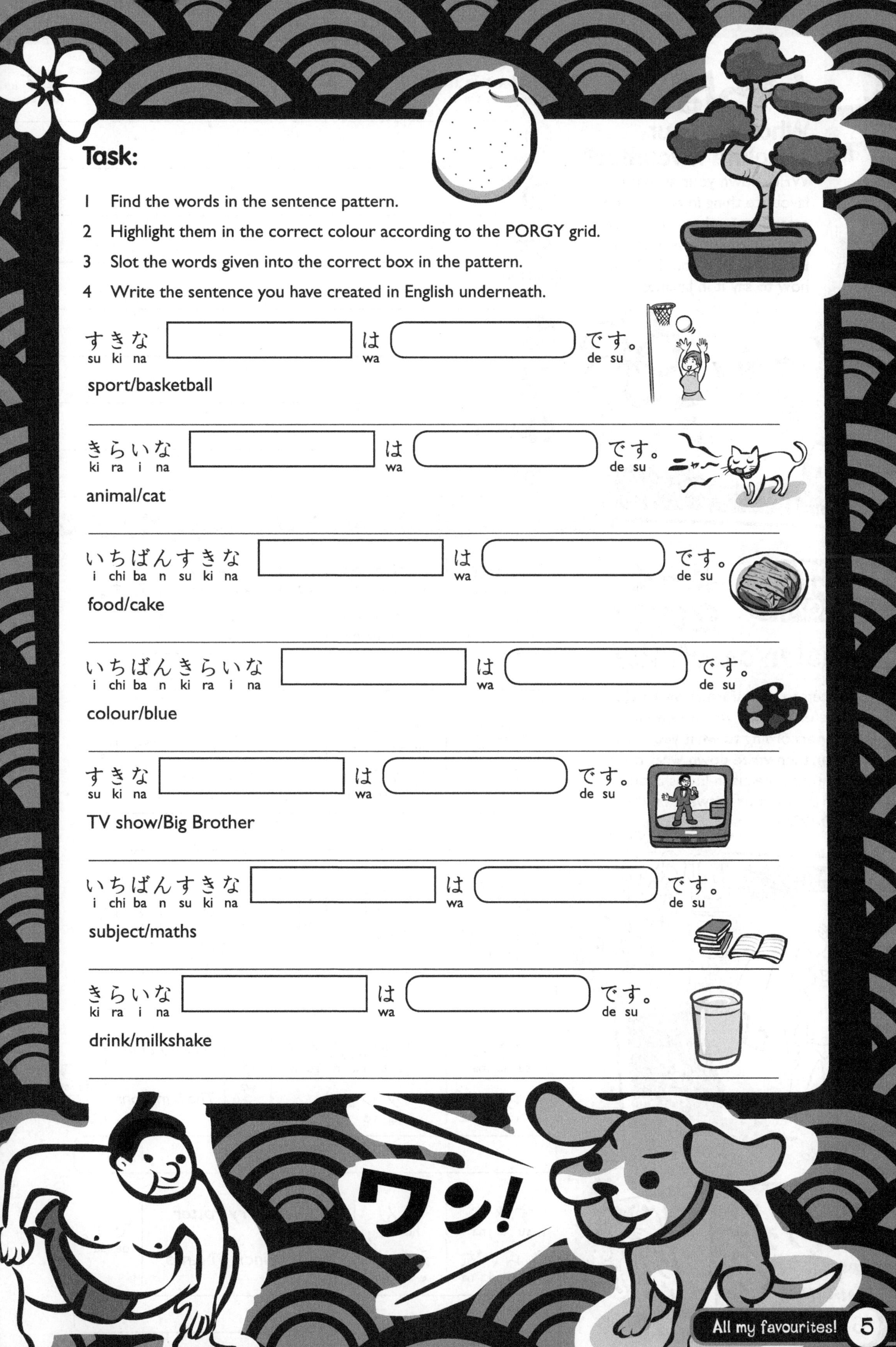

Task:

1 Find the words in the sentence pattern.
2 Highlight them in the correct colour according to the PORGY grid.
3 Slot the words given into the correct box in the pattern.
4 Write the sentence you have created in English underneath.

すきな [ ] は [ ] です。
su ki na wa de su
sport/basketball

きらいな [ ] は [ ] です。
ki ra i na wa de su
animal/cat

いちばんすきな [ ] は [ ] です。
i chi ba n su ki na wa de su
food/cake

いちばんきらいな [ ] は [ ] です。
i chi ba n ki ra i na wa de su
colour/blue

すきな [ ] は [ ] です。
su ki na wa de su
TV show/Big Brother

いちばんすきな [ ] は [ ] です。
i chi ba n su ki na wa de su
subject/maths

きらいな [ ] は [ ] です。
ki ra i na wa de su
drink/milkshake

いちばん！

What are your absolute favourites?

Write down your absolute favourite thing in each of the categories and tell your friend about it in Japanese. Use an English word if you don't know how to say it in Japanese.

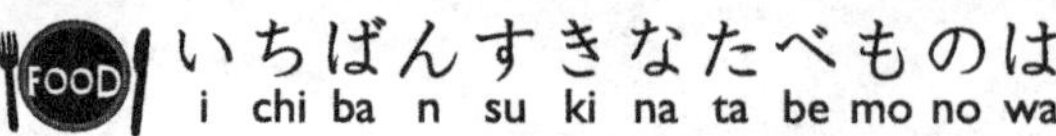

FOOD いちばんすきなたべものは ______ です。
i chi ba n su ki na ta be mo no wa ______ de su

SPORT

ANIMALS

COLOURS

SUBJECTS

TV SHOWS

MOVIES

CELEBRITY

CD ROM よーく きいて！

Listen carefully!

Listen to the information. Circle one of the two words in each pair according to what you hear, then write down what the sentence means in English. You can check your answers on the CD-ROM later.

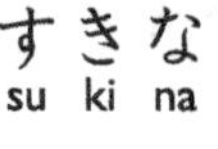

すきな su ki na / きらいな ki ra i na	たべもの ta be mo no / のみもの no mi mo no	は wa	コーラ ko o ra / すし su shi	です。 de su

______

すきな su ki na / きらいな ki ra i na	スポーツ su po o tsu / どうぶつ do u bu tsu	は wa	いぬ i nu / ラグビー ra gu bi i	です。 de su

______

すきな su ki na / きらいな ki ra i na	かもく ka mo ku / いろ i ro	は wa	すうがく su u ga ku / ピンク pi n ku	です。 de su

______

すきな su ki na / きらいな ki ra i na	テレビばんぐみ te re bi ba n gu mi / タレント ta re n to	は wa	*Hillary Duff* / *The Simpsons*	です。 de su

______

すきな su ki na / きらいな ki ra i na	ほん ho n / えいが e i ga	は wa	*Harry Potter* / *Finding Nemo*	です。 de su

______

Kana corner

Look at the new characters on the CD-ROM and practise writing them here in the correct stroke order.

ha	は	は								
ba	ば	ば								
ki	き	き								
ra	ら	ら								
ka	か	か								

Hey!

Did you know that you can write the word いちばん (*ichiban*) with the kanji 一 meaning number 1 and ばん (*ban*) in hiragana so it looks like this:

一ばん

Now you can read and write the whole sentence pattern in hiragana. If you want to write the whole sentence out you can either copy the Japanese from the word lists or you can write your answer in romaji (English writing).

See if you can read these. Use the buttons on page 2 to help you with the categories.

1. 一ばん　すきな　のみもの　は　なん　です　か。

2. 一ばん　きらいな　スポーツ　は　なん　です　か。

3. 一ばん　すきな　テレビばんぐみ　は House です。

4. 一ばん　きらいな　どうぶつ　は　へび　です。

Hiragana match-up

Match up each hiragana with its correct pronunciation by colouring them the same colour or circling them in the same way.

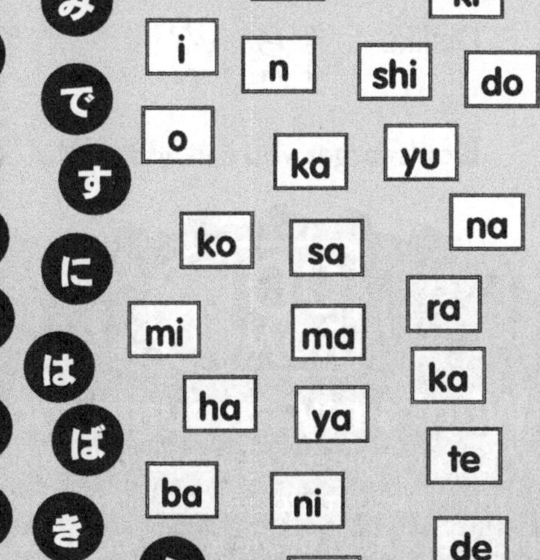

しゅくだい

HOMEWORK:

Ask your teacher for flashcards for the rest of the hiragana you have learnt so far. Colour them in and put them up in your room or on your fridge. Practise reading them every time you see them and show everyone in your house how clever you are!

Now, you choose the snack!

Now that you've got the patterns, it's up to you to choose the categories you want to talk about. If you like you can talk about them all simply by slotting the right word into the right box. You can even talk about other people's most liked and most disliked things by adding the person's name and の (*no*) to the front of the sentence. Ask your teacher for more information.

CD ROM

Hey! I can:

- ☐ **Ask someone about the things they like and dislike and answer when someone asks me**
- ☐ **Talk about the things I like and dislike**
- ☐ **Talk about my favourites**

②たべもの All about food

Word Hint でも means "but"

This is the torture page! All this talk about food and it's a long wait until lunchtime! Hang on to your tummies because it's time to talk about the foods that you love and hate.

Word Hint と means and

NEW STUFF きょうのポイント

The question:

Like すきな (su ki na) / Dislike きらいな (ki ra i na) たべもの は なん です か。 (ta be mo no wa na n de su ka)

The answer:

Like すきな (su ki na) / Dislike きらいな (ki ra i na) たべもの は ______ です。 (ta be mo no wa ... de su)

Word Hint そして means and/also

Don't forget you can add 一ばん (*ichiban*) to the front to talk about your most favourite or most hated food.

What's my favourite food?

Watch the videos of people talking about their favourite foods and draw a quick picture of each of the foods mentioned on the plates provided.

Talking about food

Vocab you might need:

やさい (ya sa i) vegetables

くだもの (ku da mo no) fruit

さかな (sa ka na) fish

ピザ (pi za) pizza

チョコレート (cho ko re e to) chocolate

アイスクリーム (a i su ku ri i mu) ice-cream

フライド ポテト (fu ra i do po te to) hot chips

サラダ (sa ra da) salad

ステーキ (su te e ki) steak

ケーキ (ke e ki) cake

パスタ (pa su ta) pasta

ハンバーガー (ha n ba a ga a) hamburgers

How does it taste?

おいしい
o i shi i

まずい
ma zu i

すっぱい
su p pa i

あまい
a ma i

からい
ka ra i

あつい
a tsu i

つめたい
tsu me ta i

Choose appropriate tastes for each of these foods and copy the word into the box provided. Then, make the comment to your friend:

________ ですね！
de su ne

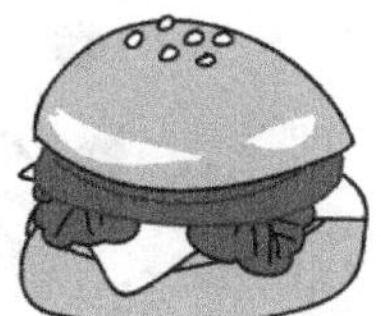

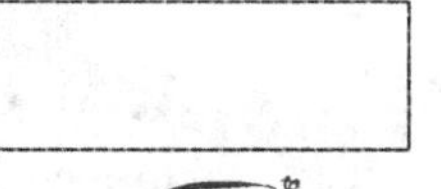

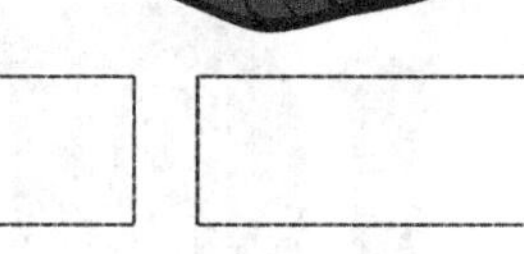

Akiko's food thoughts

Watch the video of Akiko talking about different foods. What is she saying? Link up the adjective with the food she is talking about.

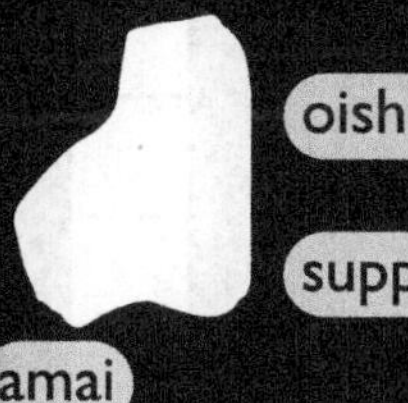

oishii

oishii

suppai

karai

amai

chotto nigai

atsui

tsumetai

mazui

Hey! That sounds familiar!

Did you notice how most of the foods in the new words list sound a bit like English? Well that's because most western foods eaten in Japan come from English. These words are called 外来語 (*gairaigo*). Ask your teacher to read these ones to you and see if you can identify them. Write them in English underneath.

カレーライス
ka re e ra i su

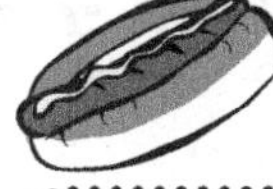
ホットドッグ
ho t to do g gu

ポーク
po o ku

ポテト・サラダ
po te to sa ra da

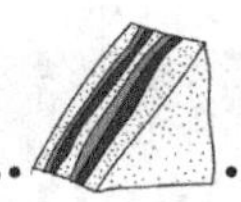
サンドイッチ
sa n do i t chi

チキン
chi ki n

ホットケーキ
ho t to ke e ki

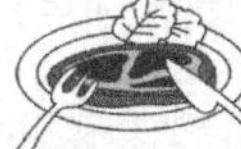
ステーキ
su te e ki

チョコレート・パフェ
cho ko re e to pa fe

ミートパイ
mi i to pa i

ビーフ
bi i fu

Read the clues in Japanese and fill in the puzzle with the English word.

よこ Across

2 ブロッコリー
bu ro k ko ri i

4 くだもの
ku da mo no

6 ステーキ
su te e ki

7 チョコレート
cho ko re e to

8 パスタ
pa su ta

9 サラダ
sa ra da

10 さかな
sa ka na

たて Down

1 ハンバーガー (more than 1)
ha n ba a ga a

3 やさい
ya sa i

5 フライド ポテト
fu ra i do po te to

7 ケーキ
ke e ki

8 ピザ
pi za

...and speaking of ice-cream...

When it comes to icecream flavours, it's easy! Most of them sound like English! With a little knowledge of katakana, or even a katakana chart hidden in your pocket, you will be able to spend many yummy hours in icecream parlours in Japan.

Listen to the following flavours and see if you can figure them out in English then, colour the cones with the appropriate colour.

Listen to the song on the CD-ROM, and then sing along!

ド・レ・ミ・ファ・そんぐ

The Yummy Yucky food song
Sing this song to the tune of *twinkle twinkle, little star*

いちばんすきな　たべものは
ichi ba n su ki na　ta be mo no wa
なんです、なんです、なんですか。
na n de su　na n de su　na n de su ka
ピッザ、チョコレート、サラダ
pi z za　cho ko re e to　sa ra da
ステーキ、ケーキ、ハンバーガー
su te e ki　ke e ki　ha n ba a ga a
いちばんすきな　たべものは
ichi ba n su ki na　ta be mo no wa
なんです、なんです、なんですか。
na n de su　na n de su　na n de su ka
ステーキ、ケーキ、ハンバーガー
su te e ki　ke e ki　ha n ba a ga a

いちばんきらいな　たべものは
ichi ba n ki ra i na　ta be mo no wa
なんです、なんです、なんですか。
na n de su　na n de su　na n de su ka
ブロッコリー、やさい、パスタ
bu ro k ko ri i　ya sa i　pa su ta
フライドポテト、チョコレート、さかな
fu ra i do po te to　cho ko re e to　sa ka na
ステーキ、ケーキ、ハンバーガー
su te e ki　ke e ki　ha n ba a ga a
いちばんきらいな　たべものは
ichi ba n ki ra i na　ta be mo no wa
なんです、なんです、なんですか。
na n de su　na n de su　na n de su ka

CD ROM Hey! I can:

- ☐ Ask someone what foods they like or don't and answer when someone asks me
- ☐ Talk about what my favourite foods are
- ☐ Comment on the tastes of certain foods
- ☐ Make Japanese ポテト・サラダ (*potato sarada*)
- ☐ Recognise the Japanese names for some foods and ice-cream flavours

しゅくだい

HOMEWORK:

You're going to make Japanese **ポテト・サラダ** (*potato sarada*). It's different to the potato salad you probably have at home. So try it!

You will need:

3 medium potatoes

1 teaspoon lemon juice

You can substitute this for 2-3 tablespoons mayonnaise

2 tablespoons sour cream

a little salt and pepper

1/2 Lebanese cucumber, thinly sliced

1/4 onion or red onion, thinly sliced

2 slices ham cut into 1 cm squares

Here's what you do:

1. Wash the potatoes thoroughly then wrap them individually in plastic wrap and cook them in the microwave for about 6 minutes.
2. Take off the wrap and peel off the skin while they are still hot. You may need to hold them in a paper towel as they will be really hot!
3. Place the potatoes in a bowl and roughly break up the potato with a wooden spoon.
4. Combine the lemon juice, sour cream and salt and pepper (to make your own 'mayonnaise').
5. Combine potato cucumber, ham and mayonnaise in a bowl.
6. Gently mix together and refrigerate. You can sprinkle with black pepper if you like.

Now, serve it for dinner and teach everyone in your household to say: **おいしい！** (*oishii!*) Deeelicious!!!

You could try eating your **ポテト・サラダ** (*potato sarada*) with chopsticks and even take some to school tomorrow for lunch!

③のみもの Drinks!

After all this hard work you must be a bit thirsty... Check out the drink menu. どうぞ！

NEW STUFF きょうのポイント

The question:

Like	すきな su ki na	のみもの は なん です か。 no mi mo no wa na n de su ka	
Dislike	きらいな ki ra i na		

Word Hint
と means **and**

The answer:

Like	すきな su ki na	のみもの は ＿＿＿＿ です。 no mi mo no wa ＿＿＿＿ de su	
Dislike	きらいな ki ra i na		

Don't forget, you can add 一ばん (*ichiban*) to the front to talk about your most favourite or most hated drink.

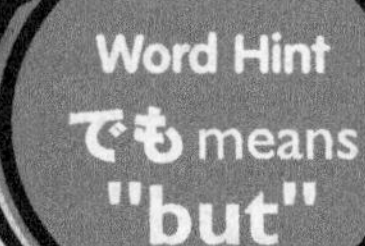

Talking about drinks

Vocab you might need:

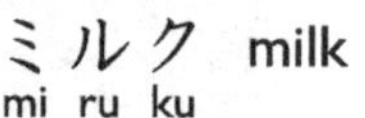

ミルク (mi ru ku) milk

みず (mi zu) water

ミルクセーキ (mi ru ku se e ki) milkshake

コーラ (ko o ra) cola

ラムネ (ra mu ne) Japanese style lemonade

オレンジ ジュース (o re n ji ju u su) orange juice

アップル ジュース (a p pu ru ju u su) apple juice

コーヒー (ko o hi i) coffee

こうちゃ (ko u cha) tea

おちゃ (o cha) green tea

カプチーノ (ka pu chi i no) cappuccino

What is ラムネ (ramune)?

It's Japanese-style lemonade. It's sweeter, a bit like lemon sherbet, and a bit more fizzy than our lemonade. And … it comes in a cool blue glass bottle. It has no lid, but is sealed with a glass ball, which you push down into it to drink it. Check it out on the CD-ROM and make sure you try one if you go to Japan.

CD ROM ペコペコカフェ Peko Peko Cafe

Listen to the drinks which you can order in the **ペコペコカフェ** (Peko Peko Cafe). Write them down in English in the space provided.

1 ______________________________

2 ______________________________

3 ______________________________

4 ______________________________

5 ______________________________

6 ______________________________

7 ______________________________

8 ______________________________

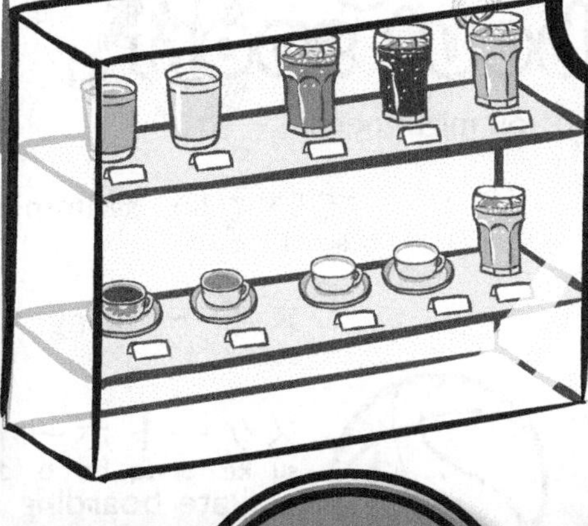

Word Hint
そして means **and/also**

Canned Coffee?

Read the article below and answer the questions.

Yes, it's true! Canned coffee is one of Japan's most popular drinks. It is available hot or cold in vending machines all over Japan. But it's not just coffee. You have a choice between café au lait, cappuccino, and many other styles.

But that's not all! Vending machines also sell a range of teas, hot chocolate, soft drinks and mineral waters. Sales of canned and bottled teas have increased dramatically over the last 10 years, even surpassing sales of soft drinks. The most popular is oolong tea, followed by black tea, green tea and barley tea. Also teas with fruit or herbs have become very popular. Sports drinks have also become popular in Japan. Pocari Sweat is the most popular brand. New jelly-style health drinks are also popular and available in vending machines. They are sold in soft packs and you squeeze them into your mouth.

1. What kinds of coffee are available in vending machines in Japan?

____

2. What other drinks are available?

____

3. What is the most popular tea sold?

____

4. What is particular about the new style of health drink?

____

CD ROM Hey! I can:

- ☐ **Ask someone what their favourite drinks are and answer when someone asks me**
- ☐ **Ask someone what drinks they don't like, and answer when someone asks me**
- ☐ **Talk about what drinks I like and dislike**
- ☐ **Talk about Japanese lemonade**
- ☐ **Talk about Japanese vending machines**

④スポーツ Sport

Hey, sports fans, it's your turn! What is your favourite sport? What sport really drives you nuts? Have you ever tried any Japanese traditional sports? Check it out on this page.

NEW STUFF きょうのポイント

Word Hint
でも means **"but"**

The question:

Like	すきな (su ki na)	スポーツ は なん です か。 (su po o tsu wa na n de su ka)
Dislike	きらいな (ki ra i na)	

The answer:

Like	すきな (su ki na)	スポーツ は ______ です。 (su po o tsu wa ... de su)
Dislike	きらいな (ki ra i na)	

Don't forget you can add 一ばん (*ichiban*) to the front to talk about your most favourite or most hated sport.

Talking about sport

Vocab you might need:

サッカー	sa k ka a	soccer
ラグビー	ra gu bi i	rugby
テニス	te ni su	tennis
ネットボール	ne t to bo o ru	netball
ホッケー	ho k ke e	hockey
すいえい	su i e i	swimming
スキー	su ki i	skiing
スケートボード	su ke e to bo o do	skate boarding
サイクリング	sa i ku ri n gu	bike riding
サーフィン	sa a fi n	surfing

What does it say?

Write the English.

いちばん　すきな　スポーツ　は　なん　です　か。
i chi ba n　su ki na　su po o tsu　wa　na n　de su　ka

すきな　スポーツ　は　すいえい　です。
su ki na　su po o tsu　wa　su i e i　de su

きらいな　スポーツ　は　サイクリング　です。
ki ra i na　su po o tsu　wa　sa i ku ri n gu　de su

いちばん　きらいな　スポーツ　は　ネットボール　です。
i chi ba n　ki ra i na　su po o tsu　wa　ne t to bo o ru　de su

いちばん　すきな　スポーツ　は　サーフィン　です。
i chi ba n　su ki na　su po o tsu　wa　sa a fi n　de su

Word Hint
と means **and**

Sport match

Listen to the CD-ROM and match up what you hear with the word and the picture.

Write the number of the item on the right hand side of the word you hear then draw a connecting line to the correct picture.

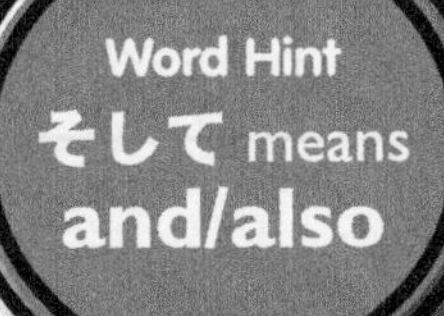

Word Hint
そして means **and/also**

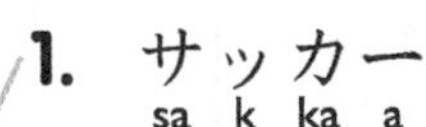

1. サッカー
sa k ka a
2. ラグビー
ra gu bi i
3. テニス
te ni su
4. ネットボール
ne t to bo o ru
5. ホッケー
ho k ke e
6. すいえい
su i e i
7. スキー
su ki i
8. スケートボード
su ke e to bo o do
9. サイクリング
sa i ku ri n gu
10. サーフィン
sa a fi n

Word Hint
でも means
"but"

What sports do you like?

CD ROM

Watch as the Japanese kids tell you what sports they like. Write them down as you hear them.

1 ______________________

2 ______________________

3 ______________________

4 ______________________

5 ______________________

Talk Time おしゃべりタイム

Survey your classmates and find out the most popular sport in your class.

Make a graph of your findings by colouring a bar for each vote. Then write the totals for each sport in kanji at the bottom.

Using the graph answer these questions in Japanese.

Which is the most popular sport? ______________________

Which is the least popular sport? ______________________

How many people were surveyed altogether? ______________________

Word Hint
そして means
and/also

XTRA STUFF もっともっと

CD ROM

すきなスポーツはなんですか。
suki na supootsu wa nan desu ka

What sport do you play?
どんな スポーツ を し ますか
do n na su po o tsu o shi ma su ka?

Sport を しますか。
o shi ma su ka
Do you play sport?

Sport を します。
I play sport.

Sport を しません。
I don't play sport.

Tell your friend what sports you play and ask them what they play.

Word Hint
と means and

Japanese traditional sports

CD ROM

Can you name these traditional sports of Japan? Write the name underneath each photo. You can get more information about these on the CD-ROM.

kendo / judo / aikido / sumo / karate / kyudo

Sumo Match

Check out for instructions for making your own Sumo game and then play it with your friends. Ask your teacher!

しゅくだい

HOMEWORK:

Jump on the internet and find out if it is possible to learn one of the Japanese traditional martial arts in your area. Find out where, what day of the week and how much it costs.

Hey! I can:

CD ROM

- ☐ Ask someone what their favourite sports are and answer when someone asks me
- ☐ Ask someone what sports they don't like, and answer when someone asks me
- ☐ Talk about what sports I like and dislike
- ☐ Talk about traditional sports
- ☐ Talk about what sports I play and don't play

⑤いろ Colours

Get out those coloured pencils, because it's time to talk about colours.

NEW STUFF きょうのポイント

Word Hint
と means **and**

The question:

Like すきな (su ki na) / Dislike きらいな (ki ra i na) いろ は なん です か。 (i ro wa na n de su ka)

The answer:

Like すきな (su ki na) / Dislike きらいな (ki ra i na) いろ は ______ です。 (i ro wa ... de su)

Don't forget, you can add 一ばん (*ichiban*) to the front to talk about your most favourite or most hated colours.

Word Hint
でも means **"but"**

Talking about colours

Vocab you might need:

あか (a ka) red	くろ (ku ro) black
あお (a o) blue	オレンジ (o re n ji) orange
きいろ (ki i ro) yellow	ピンク (pi n ku) pink
みどり (mi do ri) green	むらさき (mu ra sa ki) purple
しろ (shi ro) white	ちゃいろ (cha i ro) brown

What's your favourite colour?

1. Write a sentence stating the colours you like.

2. Write a sentence stating the colours you dislike.

3. Write a sentence stating the colour you like the most.

4. Write a sentence stating the colour you dislike the most.

5. Ask three friends what colour they like most and dislike most. Write their names and what they answered.

6. Find someone in your class whose favourite colour is the same as yours. Write their name here.

7. Find someone in your class whose most hated colour is the same as yours. Write their name here.

SING **CD ROM** Listen to the song on the CD-ROM, and then sing along!

ド・レ・ミ・ファ・そんぐ

The greetings song to the tune of *I Can Sing a Rainbow*

Try singing the first verse of *I can sing a Rainbow* in Japanese. Sing along with the CD-ROM.

あか、きいろ、みどり a ka ki i ro mi do ri	しろ、ピンク、ちゃいろ、 shi ro pi n ku cha i ro
むらさき、あお mu ra sa ki a o	オレンジ、くろ o re n ji ku ro
にじがみえる、 ni ji ga mi e ru	にじがみえる、 ni ji ga mi e ru
みえる mi e ru	みえる mi e ru
みえるよ。 mi e ru yo	みえるよ。 mi e ru yo

Word Hint
そして means **and/also**

The Colours of Japan

Look at the photos of Japan on the CD-ROM and colour each of the pictures the correct colour.

Classroom colours

Find the following objects in the classroom, colour them the right colour and write the colour in the box.

GAMES 4 U 2 PLAY

はやくちことば
Tongue twister

あかパジャマ red pajamas
a ka pa ja ma

きパジャマ yellow pajamas
ki pa ja ma

ちゃパジャマ brown pajamas
cha pa ja ma

しゅくだい
HOMEWORK:

Choose 9 of the 10 colours you have learnt and make a Reveal-a-Picture Puzzle. The pattern and the instructions are on the CD-ROM. Then bring it to school and have your friends try to do it.

CD ROM Hey! I can:

- ☐ Ask someone what their favourite colours are and answer when someone asks me
- ☐ Ask someone what colour they don't like, and answer when someone asks me
- ☐ Talk about what colours I like and dislike
- ☐ Sing a song about colours
- ☐ Recognise different Japanese images and what colours they are
- ☐ Say a Japanese tongue twister

⑥ どうぶつ Animals

Are you an animal lover? Or do you hate anything to do with fur, feathers and fins? Well, here's your chance to have your say. Tell us about the animals you love to love and love to hate.

NEW STUFF きょうのポイント

The question:

Like すきな (su ki na) / Dislike きらいな (ki ra i na) どうぶつ は なん です か。 (do u bu tsu wa na n de su ka)

The answer:

Like すきな (su ki na) / Dislike きらいな (ki ra i na) どうぶつ は ______ です。 (do u bu tsu wa ______ de su)

Don't forget, you can add 一ばん (*ichiban*) to the front to talk about your most favourite or most hated animals.

Talking about animals

Vocab you might need:

いぬ (i nu)	dog	ねずみ (ne zu mi)	mouse
ねこ (ne ko)	cat	へび (he bi)	snake
うま (u ma)	horse	とり (to ri)	bird
うさぎ (u sa gi)	rabbit	きんぎょ (ki n gyo)	goldfish
コアラ (ko a ra)	koala	かえる (ka e ru)	frog
カンガルー (ka n ga ru u)	kangaroo	あひる (a hi ru)	duck

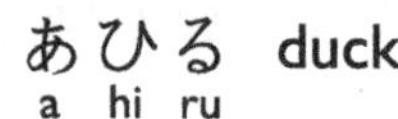

XTRA STUFF もっともっと

CD ROM

おおきい big
o o ki i

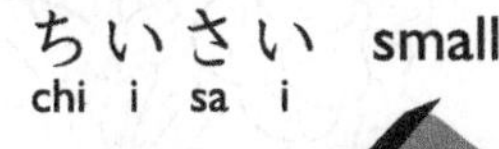

ちいさい small
chi i sa i

かわいい cute
ka wa i i

こわい scary
ko wa i

What are these people saying?

いちばん すきな
i chi ba n su ki na
どうぶつ は
do u bu tsu wa
かえる です。
ka e ru de su

What's your favourite animal?

Draw a picture of your favourite animal and write a sentence about it in Japanese.

Identify the animal

CD ROM

Listen to the CD-ROM and identify the animal words. Write down the animal in English as you hear it and draw a picture in the box.

1 ____________________

2 ____________________

3 ____________________

4 ____________________

5 ____________________

Find-a-pet

All the pets have been lost in the jungle. Look if you find some of the missing pets and colour them in. Circle the ones you find.

いぬ i nu	コアラ ko a ra	とり to ri
ねこ ne ko	カンガルー ka n ga ru u	きんぎょ ki n gyo
うま u ma	ねずみ ne zu mi	かえる ka e ru
うさぎ u sa gi	へび he bi	あひる a hi ru

Animal sounds

Listen to the CD-ROM to hear the animal sounds then write in Japanese what animal you hear.

1 ____________ 6 ____________

2 ____________ 7 ____________

3 ____________ 8 ____________

4 ____________

5 ____________

Origami rabbit

Ask your teacher how to make an origami rabbit.

Hey! Did you know that there are some animals and creatures which feature in Japanese folktales? Check them out and then label them with the correct name.

CD ROM

What am I?

Read the clue and identify the animal. Write its name in the boxes provided and draw a picture of it. You can write them in romaji or kana or both.

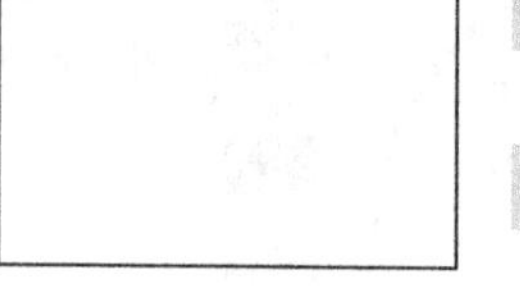

Hint 1: いけにすんでいます。
i ke ni su n de i ma su

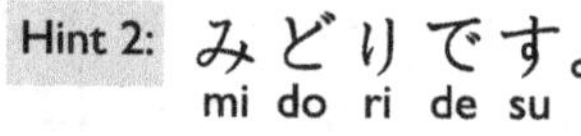

Hint 2: みどりです。
mi do ri de su

New vocab
いけ pond
i ke

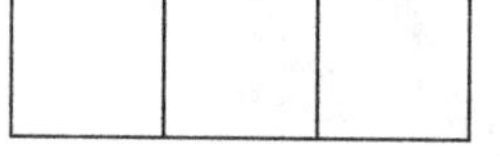

Hint 3: ケロケロ。
ke ro ke ro

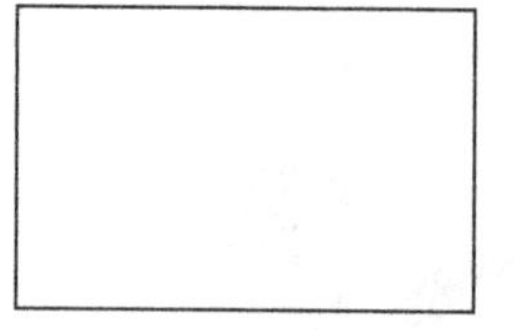

Hint 1: おおきいです。
o o ki i de su

Hint 2: しろ／くろ／ちゃいろです。
shi ro ku ro cha i ro de su

Hint 3: ヒヒーン
hi hi i n

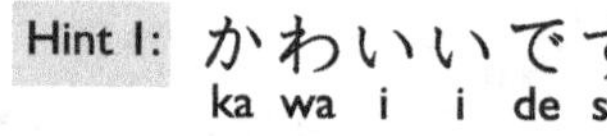

Hint 1: かわいいです。
ka wa i i de su

Hint 2: すきなたべものはやさいです。
su ki na ta be mo no wa ya sa i de su

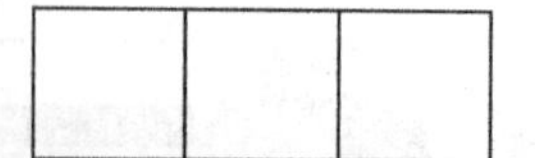

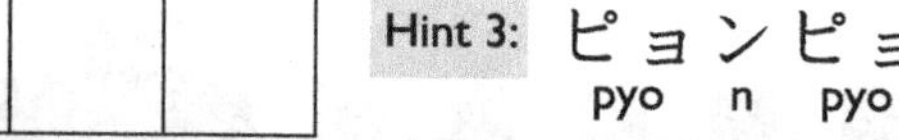

Hint 3: ピョンピョン
pyo n pyo n

ド・レ・ミ・ファ・そんぐ

CD ROM **Song to the tune of *'Old McDonald Had a Farm'***

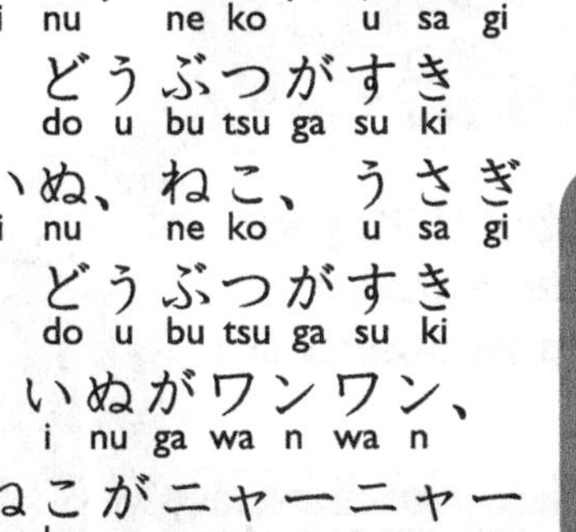

いぬ、ねこ、うさぎ
i nu ne ko u sa gi
どうぶつがすき
do u bu tsu ga su ki
いぬ、ねこ、うさぎ
i nu ne ko u sa gi
どうぶつがすき
do u bu tsu ga su ki
いぬがワンワン、
i nu ga wa n wa n
ねこがニャーニャー
ne ko ga nya a nya a
ワンワンニャーニャー、
wa n wa n nya a nya a
うさぎがピョンピョン
u sa gi ga pyo n pyo n
いぬ、ねこ、うさぎ
i nu ne ko u sa gi
どうぶつがすき
do u bu tsu ga su ki

うま、きんぎょ、ねずみ、
u ma ki n gyo ne zu mi
どうぶつがすき
do u bu tsu ga su ki
うま、きんぎょ、ねずみ、
u ma ki n gyo ne zu mi
どうぶつがすき
do u bu tsu ga su ki
うまがヒーヒン、きんぎょがスイスイ
u ma ga hi i hi n ki n gyo ga su i su i
ヒーヒン、スイスイ、
hi i hi n su i su i
ねずみがチューチュー
ne zu mi ga chu u chu u
うま、きんぎょ、ねずみ、
u ma ki n gyo ne zu mi
どうぶつがすき
do u bu tsu ga su ki

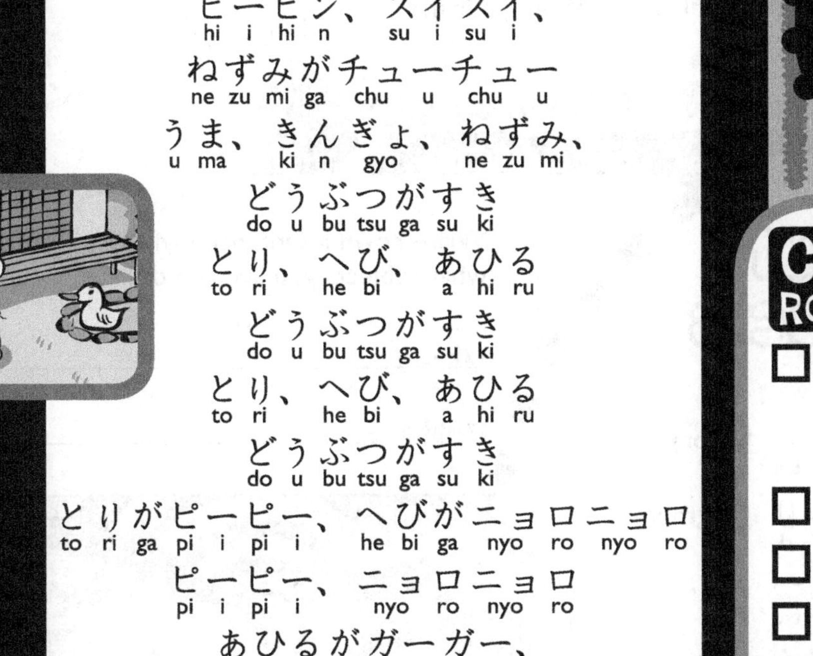

とり、へび、あひる
to ri he bi a hi ru
どうぶつがすき
do u bu tsu ga su ki
とり、へび、あひる
to ri he bi a hi ru
どうぶつがすき
do u bu tsu ga su ki
とりがピーピー、へびがニョロニョロ
to ri ga pi i pi i he bi ga nyo ro nyo ro
ピーピー、ニョロニョロ
pi i pi i nyo ro nyo ro
あひるがガーガー、
a hi ru ga ga a ga a
とり、へび、あひる
to ri he bi a hi ru
どうぶつがすき
do u bu tsu ga su ki
えっ！へび？！！！こわーい！！！
e he bi ko wa a i

CD ROM **Here is a well-known song about a frog. Listen to it and sing along.**

かえるのうた

The Frog Song

かえるのうたが
ka e ru no u ta ga
The frog's song
きこえてくるよ
ki ko e te ku ru yo
can be heard

クァ、クァ、クァ、クァ
kwa kwa kwa kwa
croak, croak, croak, croak
ケロ、ケロ、ケロ、ケロ
ke ro ke ro ke ro ke ro
ribit, ribit, ribit. ribit
クァ、クァ、クァ
kwa kwa kwa
croak, croak, croak

しゅくだい

HOMEWORK:

Find a photo of your pet or your favourite animal, Attach it to a piece of cardboard and write a caption underneath in Japanese.

CD ROM **Hey! I can:**

- ☐ Ask someone what animals they like and answer when someone asks me
- ☐ Talk about my favourite animals
- ☐ Make animal sounds in Japanese
- ☐ Sing two new songs
- ☐ Talk about animals in some Japanese folktales

⑦ かもく School subjects

It's the topic most teachers are too afraid to talk about! it's your favourite subject and – even worse – your favourite teacher! Here's your chance to have your say. Forget the consequences! Just say it ... but say it in Japanese!

NEW STUFF きょうのポイント

The question:

Like すきな (su ki na) / Dislike きらいな (ki ra i na) かもく は なん です か。 (ka mo ku wa na n de su ka)

The answer:

Like すきな (su ki na) / Dislike きらいな (ki ra i na) かもく は 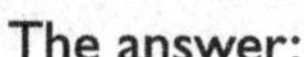 です。 (ka mo ku wa ... de su)

Don't forget, you can add 一ばん (*ichiban*) to the front to talk about your most favourite or most hated subject.

Talking about school subjects

Vocab you might need:

こくご (ko ku go) English

すうがく (su u ga ku) or さんすう (sa n su) maths

りか (ri ka) science

しゃかい (sha ka i) social studies/civics/HSIE

たいいく (ta i i ku) PE

れきし (re ki shi) history

ちり (chi ri) geography

びじゅつ (bi ju tsu) art

おんがく (o n ga ku) music

日本ご (ni hon go) Japanese

かていか (ka te i ka) Home science

Write down a sentence saying what subjects you like and dislike.

Like: ____________________

Dislike: ____________________

おしゃべりタイム
Talk Time

Ask three people about their favourite subjects and complete the sentences with the information.

Question:

いちばん すきな かもく は なん です か。
i chi ba n su ki na ka mo ku wa na n de su ka

Friend's name 1 さん の いちばん すきな かもく は ______ です。
sa n no i chi ba n su ki na ka mo ku wa de su

Friend's name 2 さん の いちばん すきな かもく は ______ です。
sa n no i chi ba n su ki na ka mo ku wa de su

Friend's name 3 さん の いちばん すきな かもく は ______ です。
sa n no i chi ba n su ki na ka mo ku wa de su

Write down the names of 2 people in the class who gave the same answer.

かもく ______ なまえ 1 ______ なまえ 2 ______

Choose the correct word

Circle the word you hear, and write the number next the right picture.

1 りか (ri ka)
2 おんがく (o n ga ku)
3 日本ご (ni hon go)
4 こくご (ko ku go)
5 れきし (re ki shi)
6 びじゅつ (bi ju tsu)
7 すうがく (su u ga ku)
8 ちり (chi ri)

Secret subjects

Unjumble these words to reveal the secret subjects then write すき next to it if you like it and きらい next to it if you don't like it.

じゅつび (ju tsu bi) ______ ( )
がくすう (ga ku su u) ______ ( )
かり (ka ri) ______ ( )
れしき (re shi ki) ______ ( )
くごこ (ku go ko) ______ ( )
んくがお (n ku ga o) ______ ( )
かいしゃ (ka i sha) ______ ( )
ごほんに (go ho n ni) ______ ( )
りち (ri chi) ______ ( )

Hey! The word こくご (*kokugo*) really means the language of our country, so for us *kokugo* is English, but for Japanese kids *kokugo* is Japanese, and they call English えいご (*eigo*).

Rank your subjects

Copy out your list of subjects in Japanese in two groups, those you like and those you don't like. Within each list try to put them in your order of preference.

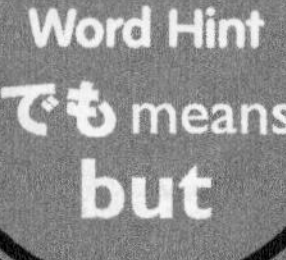

Word Hint
と means **and**

すきなかもく	きらいなかもく

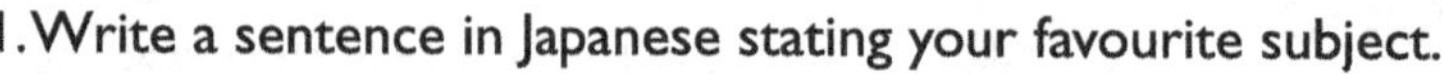

1. Write a sentence in Japanese stating your favourite subject.

Word Hint
そして means
and also

2. Write a sentence in Japanese stating the subject you dislike the most.

Days of the week
Check out the CD-ROM if you want to know how to write the days of the week.

Timetable

Fill in your school timetable in Japanese by adding the times of each lesson, your subjects, and recess (きゅうけいじかん *kyuukei jikan*) and lunchtime (ひるやすみ *hiru yasumi*). If you do a sport or an activity after school you can add it at the bottom.

My timetable

times	日	月	火	水	木	金

せんせい Teachers

The question:

すきな　せんせい　は　だれ　です　か。
su ki na　se n se i　wa　da re　de su　ka

The answer:

すきな　せんせい　は　＿＿＿＿　です。
su ki na　se n se i　wa　＿＿＿＿　de su

When you want to talk about teachers you just have to say their names in English because they are all just names and they don't change. Of course, a Japanese person would say them with a Japanese accent. Don't forget to put せんせい (*sensei*) on the end of the teacher's name.

Class survey: the most popular teacher in school

Survey your classmates in Japanese to find out their favourite teacher. The survey must remain anonymous! No students' names are to be recorded. Write down the name of any teacher who is nominated and tally their votes after that.

The Most Popular Teacher in School

せんせい の なまえ (se n se i no na ma e)	Tally	Total

and the award goes to:

School in Japan

Check out the information about school in Japan then choose the correct answer.

The Japanese school year begins in
- January
- April

Japanese 6 week summer holiday is in
- March-April
- July- August

School usually starts around
- 7:30
- 8:30

In Japanese classes there are usually
- 20-30 students
- 30-40 students

High School students wear
- dark coloured school uniforms
- anything they like

As soon as they get to school students
- clean the classrooms
- change their shoes

Primary school students
- have a hot lunch
- bring a packed lunch (obento) from home

Towards the end of the day students
- clean up their classrooms
- clean the toilets

After school students
- do club activities at school
- study for exams at school

If there is an earthquake students must
- get under a table
- hold onto their friend's legs

しゅくだい HOMEWORK:

Label each of your school books with your name and the subject in Japanese.

Hey! I can:

- ☐ Ask someone what their favourite subjects are and answer when someone asks me
- ☐ Ask someone what subjects they don't like, and answer when someone asks me
- ☐ Write out your timetable in Japanese
- ☐ Ask someone who their favourite teachers are and answer when someone asks me
- ☐ Talk about school in Japan

⑧エンターテインメント That's Entertainment!

It's time for all the glitz and glamour of the red carpet! Here's your chance to come up with your favourites in the world of entertainment. Talk about your favourite TV shows, movies and celebrities. It's the Obento Snack Pack Entertainment Awards!

NEW STUFF きょうのポイント

The question:

Like	すきな テレビばんぐみ su ki na te re bi ba n gu mi	は なん です か。 wa na n de su ka
Dislike	きらいな えいが ki ra i na e i ga	は なん です か。 wa na n de su ka
Like	すきな タレント su ki na ta re n to	は だれ です か。 wa da re de su ka

The answer:

Like	すきな テレビばんぐみ su ki na te re bi ba n gu mi	は ______ です。 wa de su
Dislike	きらいな えいが ki ra i na e i ga	は ______ です。 wa de su
Like	すきな タレント su ki na ta re n to	は ______ です。 wa de su

Don't forget, you can add 一ばん (*ichiban*) to the front to talk about your most favourite or most hated programs.

テレビばんぐみ (te re bi ba n gu mi) television programme

えいが (e i ga) movie

タレント (ta re n to) celebrity

My entertainment

When you want to talk about TV shows, movies or celebrities you just have to say them in English. They are all just names, so they don't change. Of course if you heard a Japanese person saying them, they would say them with a Japanese accent. Ask your teacher to say them for you if you like. You can either imitate their pronunciation or you can just say it in English.

Write down the shows you want to talk about on the lines provided.

____

____

Write down the movies you want to talk about on the lines provided.

____

____

Write down the celebrities you want to talk about on the lines provided.

____

____

Japanese TV on YouTube

Check out YouTube to see some funny Japanese TV programs.

Talk Time おしゃべりタイム

Nominations are open for the Obento Snack Pack Entertainment Awards. Fill out the nomination form with the best and the worst in each category, then compare your nominations with your friends. Ask five people around the room what they think. Don't forget, you must ask in Japanese!

テレビばんぐみ

一ばん　すきな　テレビばんぐみ　は ______________ です。
ichi ba n su ki na te re bi ba n gu mi wa de su

一ばん　きらいな　テレビばんぐみ　は ______________ です。
ichi ba n ki ra i na te re bi ba n gu mi wa de su

えいが

一ばん　すきな　えいが　は ______________ です。
ichi ba n su ki na e i ga wa de su

いちばん　きらいな　えいが　は ______________ です。
i chi ba n ki ra i na e i ga wa de su

タレント

一ばん　すきな　タレント　は ______________ です。
ichi ba n su ki na ta re n to wa de su

一ばん　きらいな　タレント　は ______________ です。
ichi ba n ki ra i na ta re n to wa de su

Name that celebrity!

CD ROM

GAMES 4 U 2 PLAY

CD ROM

Takeshi's Castle and Spirited Away

What is Takeshi's Castle? And what is Spirited Away? This, and other exciting questions, will be answered on the CD-ROM.

The teacher will give you the clues one by one IN JAPANESE.
If your team guesses correctly you gain 10 points.
You can guess at any time but each team will only get 5 guesses.
If you guess correctly after the first clue, you will receive a bonus 10 points.
If you guess correctly after the second clue, you will receive a bonus 8 points.
If you guess correctly after the third clue, you will receive a bonus 6 points.
If you guess correctly after the forth clue, you will receive a bonus 4 points.
The last clue is a photo of the celebrity.
ALL GUESSES MUST BE IN JAPANESE!
THE TEACHER'S DECISION IS FINAL!

You will be given five clues:

1 male/female
2 actor/singer/TV personality
3 age
4 where they live
5 a photo

But for this you will need some word help.

Gender

Male 男（おとこ）
o to ko

Female 女（おんな）
o n na

It is ____________ です。
de su

So you can say:

おとこです。 It is a male.
o to ko de su

おんなです。 It is a female.
o n na de su

Age

refresh your memory.

age さいです。 He/she is age years old.
sa i de su

So you can say:

二十三さいです。 He/she is 23 years old.
ni juu san sa i de su

Job

はいゆう actor
ha i yu u

かしゅ singer
ka shu

テレビタレント TV personality
te re bi ta re n to

____________ です。 It is
de su

So you can say:

はいゆうです。 It is an actor.
ha i yu u de su

Where they live

refresh your memory.

place にすんでいます。 He/she lives in place.
ni su n de i ma su

So you can say:

オーストラリアにすんでいます。
o o su to ra ri a ni su n de i ma su

He/she lives in Australia.

You'll find some celebrity info cards on the CD-ROM or you can make your own for your favourite celebs!

Talking about celebrities...

When you want to talk about celebrities you just have to say their names in English because they are all just names so they don't change. Of course, if you heard a Japanese person saying them they would say them with a Japanese accent. Ask your teacher to say them for you if you like. You can either imitate their pronunciation or you can just say it in English but don't forget to put さん (*san*) on the end of the celebrity's name.

Japanese celebrities

Check out the internet for information on Japanese celebrities:

Singers:

Actors:

Sports people:

Choose one Japanese celebrity and prepare a PowerPoint presentation of six slides about them and their achievements.

Reading corner

Look at the new characters on the CD-ROM and check out the two characters you have used for the celebrity game!

Read these two characters.

男	女
otoko	onna
This means 'male'.	This means 'female'.

しゅくだい

HOMEWORK:

Ask a home if you can hire a Japanese animated movie from the video shop. Watch the movie and prepare a short talk about the movie for your class.

Hey! I can:

- ☐ Ask someone what their favourite TV shows, movies and celebrities are and answer when someone asks me
- ☐ Ask someone which ones they don't like, and answer when someone asks me
- ☐ Talk about what TV shows, movies and celebrities I like and dislike
- ☐ Talk about Japanese TV shows
- ☐ Talk about Japanese movies
- ☐ Talk about famous Japanese people

⑨こどもせいかつ
It's a kid's life

Hi! I'm Shun Takahashi. I'm 11 years old. I live in a suburb of Tokyo called Koganei. I go to Tokyo Gakugei Daigaku Koganei Primary School. My favourite subject is history and my favourite sport is soccer. But hey! Come with me and I'll show you my house and my school and I'll introduce you to my family. C'mon, let's go!

6:30 AM

おはよう
o ha yo u

六じはん に おきます
roku ji ha n ni o ki ma su

AROUND THE HOUSE!
Look at Shun's house in this video.

せいふく を きます
se i fu ku o ki ma su

なんじですか？
What time is it?

Say the times on these clocks.

1 ____________________

2 ____________________

3 ____________________

4 ____________________

5 ____________________

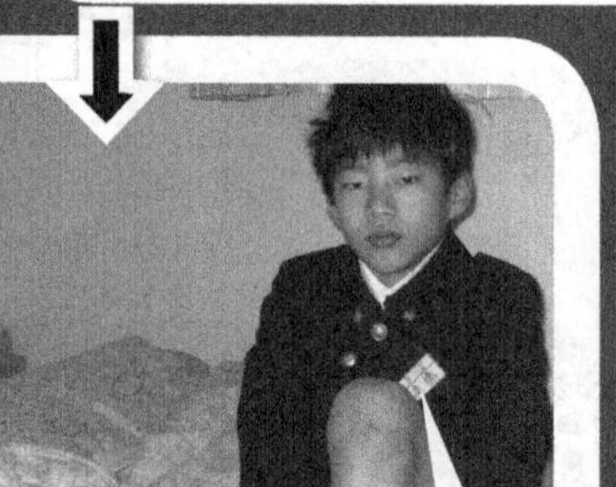

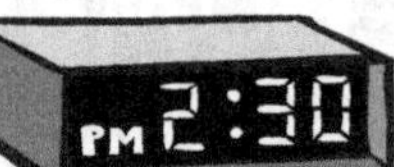

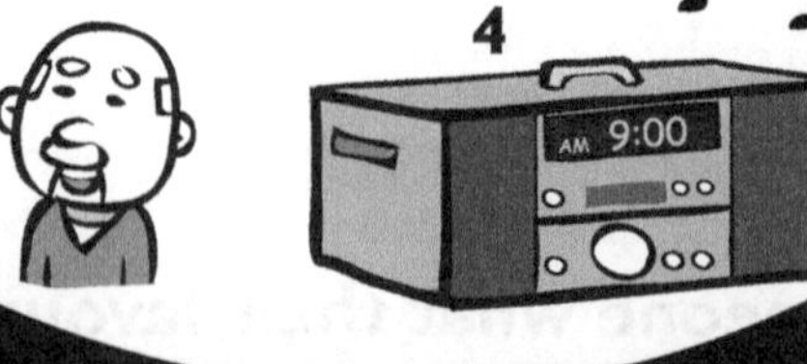

Bath Time
Check out the CD for info about taking off your shoes and having a bath. Then draw some slippers in your exercise book.

7:00 AM

七じ に
shichi ji ni
あさごはん を
a sa go ha n o
たべます
ta be ma su

いただきます
i ta da ki ma su

7:30 AM

がっこう に いきます
ga k ko u ni i ki ma su

NEW STUFF きょうのポイント

Talking about time

Number ＋ じに (ji ni)	At (number) o'clock
Number ＋ じはんに (ji ha n ni)	At half past (number)

Talk Time おしゃべりタイム

Tell your friend about your daily routine (just the morning and afternoon).

しゅんくんのへや Shun's Room

Look at the photo of Shun's room on the CD-ROM. Then grab a partner and draw a map of what you notice.

Word Hint
4 o'clock is said *yo ji*
7 o'clock is said shi *chi ji*
9 o'clock is said *ku ji*

しゅくだい HOMEWORK:

Explain to your family how to have a bath Japanese style, then ask if you can do it.

Hey! I can:

- ☐ Talk about my daily life in Japanese
- ☐ Talk about things that kids do in Japan
- ☐ Talk about time
- ☐ Talk about taking shoes off and having a bath

⑩ うちで Hanging around the house

ようこそ！**Welcome to my house. Come on in but don't forget to take your shoes off!**

CD ROM

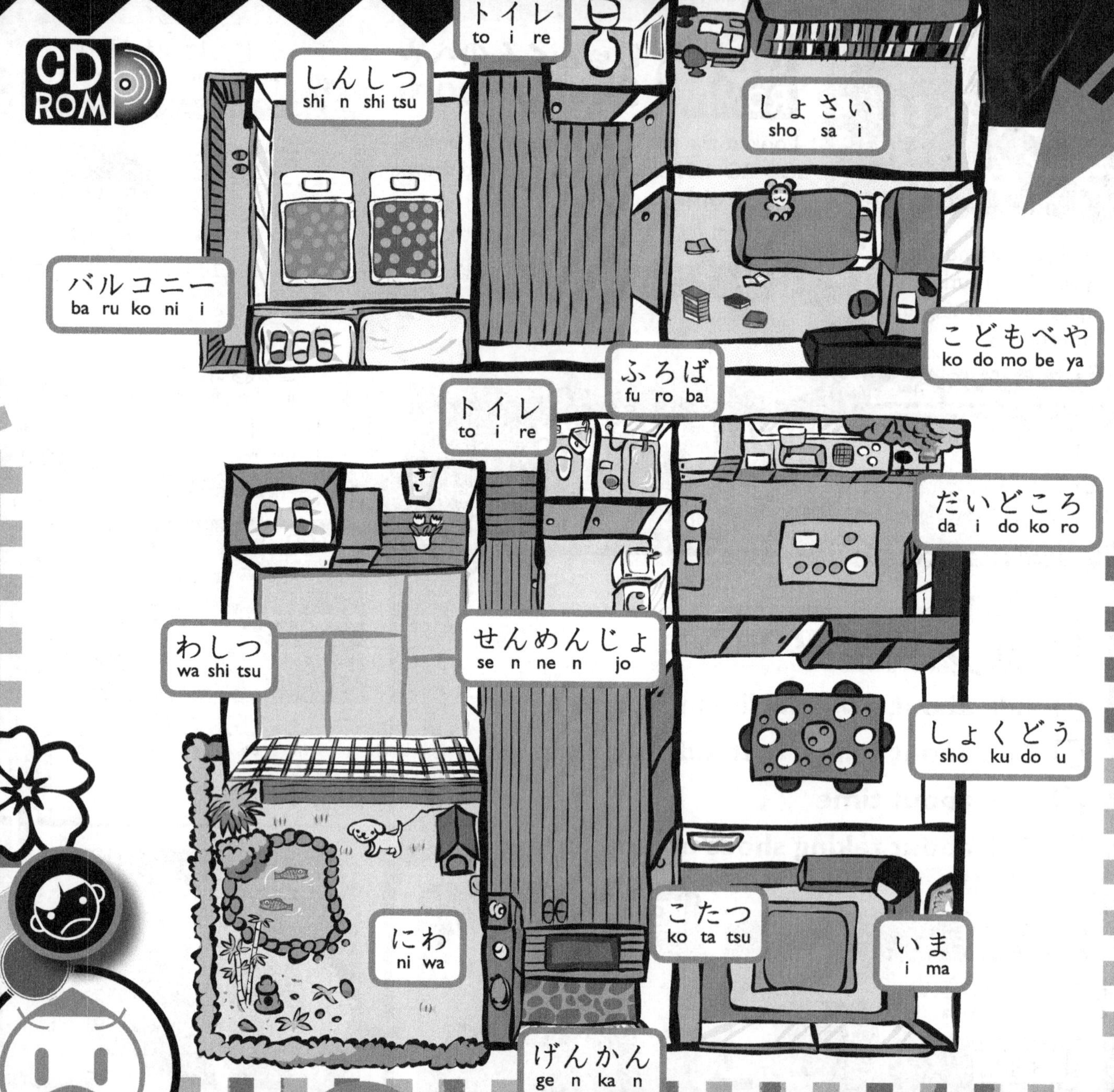

CD ROM **NEW STUFF** きょうのポイント

room に thing があります。 In the room there is a thing.
ni ga a ri ma su

Things around the house

Look at the photos of Shun s house on the CD, find these household items on the map of the house and colour them.

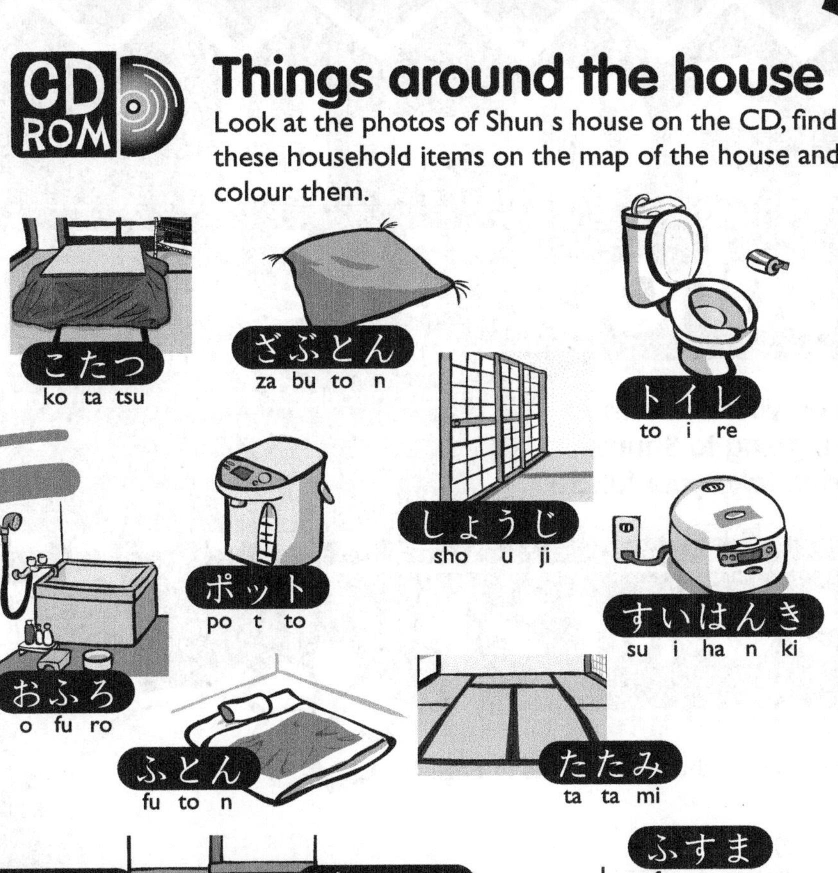

House Rules

一 Before you enter a Japanese house you must

(a) take off your hat
(b) take off your shoes
(c) wash your feet

二 Inside a Japanese house you should wear

(a) slippers
(b) thongs
(c) no shoes at all

三 Before entering a tatami room what must you do?

____

四 When sitting in a Japanese style room you would usually sit on

(a) a lounge chair
(b) a kotatsu
(c) a zabuton

五 A すいはんき (su i ha n ki) is used for:

(a) storing hot water for tea
(b) cooking rice
(c) storing futon

Toilet talk トイレのこと

Check out the CD and draw a traditional Japanese toilet and a modern Japanese toilet.

しゅくだい

HOMEWORK:

Check out the CD-ROM and make yourself some origami slippers.

Shun's house

Go on a guided tour of Shun's house as he tells you what belongs where.

Hey! I can:

- ☐ Name the rooms in a Japanese house
- ☐ Name some household items
- ☐ Say where things are kept in the house
- ☐ Talk about some customs inside the house

⑪ がっこうの一日

A day at school

C'mon, get up! It's a school day. Put on your uniform, grab your bag and your books, we're going to Shun's school. Oh, and you don't even need to take your lunch!

おべんとうをみせて！
Show us your lunch!

Form groups of 4 people and find out what each person has for lunch. Do these foods come from a particular culture?

NEW STUFF きょうのポイント

Learn the new stuff from the CD-ROM then write these sentences in English.

どこのがっこうにいっていますか。
do ko no ga k ko u ni i t te i ma su ka ______

Yamaguchi Primary School にいっています。
ni i t te i ma su ______

なんねんせいですか。
na n ne n se i de su ka ______

五ねんせいです。
go ne n se i de su ______

六ねんせいです。
roku ne n se i de su ______

七ねんせいです。
nana ne n se i de su ______

八ねんせいです。
hachi ne n se i de su ______

日本ごをべんきょうしています。
ni hon go o be n kyo u shi te i ma su ______

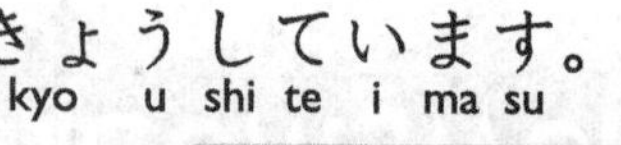

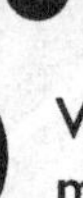

School uniforms

Check out the CD-ROM for info on school in Japan and while you're there look at the photos of the school uniforms and draw the one you like the best. Why did you choose that one? How do think it would feel to wear it to school everyday?

Vocab you might need:

こくご ko ku go ______	しゃかい sha ka i ______	おんがく o n ga ku ______
すうがく or さんすう su u ga ku sa n su u ______	れきし re ki shi ______	日本ご ni hon go ______
______	ちり chi ri ______	たいいく ta i i ku ______
りか ri ka ______	びじゅつ bi ju tsu ______	かていか ka te i ka ______

GAMES 4 U 2 PLAY

School day dictionary

What do these words mean? Find the correspondent pictures hideen in these pages.

- ホームルーム ho o mu ru u mu
- せんせい se n se i
- おべんとう o be n to u
- おそうじ o so u ji
- きゅうけいじかん kyu u ke i ji ka n
- ひるやすみ hi ru ya su mi
- じゅぎょう ju gyo u
- きょうしつ kyo u shi tsu
- きゅうしょく kyu u sho ku
- しゅくだい shu ku da i
- クラブかつどう ku ra bu ka tsu do u

O or X? The same or different?

Watch the video on schools in Japan and write whether it is the same (○) as your school or different (×). Then write how it is different.

	Same or Different	How?
Uniform		
Getting to school		
School hours		
Subjects learnt		
Recess		
Lunchtime		
Cleaning up		
After school activities		

Mystery word

Write the words in Japanese. Then unjumble the circled letters to reveal what most kids hate doing.

- school cleaning
- staffroom
- home room
- recess
- lesson
- club activities
- lunchtime
- classroom

And the answer is: ______________________

CD ROM おべんとうのこと All about obento

Find out all about obento on the CD-ROM, then write the answers these questions.

1. What is obento?
2. Where can you eat obento?
3. What kinds of foods does it contain?
4. What food do you always find in an obento?
5. What is Ekiben?
6. Traditionally, what do you eat obento with?
7. In Japan who usually makes your obento for lunch?
8. Name 3 kinds of obento.

Word Jumble

Colour in all of the letters that are listed 3 times, then unjumble the remaining letters to reveal the mystery word.

I	O	P	T	K
U	S	A	U	M
T	M	R	S	O
A	P	E	U	P
E	K	R	N	M
R	O	K	T	A

CD ROM Hey! I can:

- ☐ Say what school I go to and what year I'm in
- ☐ Say what subjects I study
- ☐ Talk about what school is like in Japan
- ☐ Talk about Japanese school lunches

⑫こどものあそび
Secret kids' business

Kids in Japan play games at school just like kids here. Put down your pens and pack up your books because this page is all about playing games. Check out the CD-ROM for the rules and a video, then drag your teacher out into the playground to play some of these games.

NEW STUFF きょうのポイント

Listen and repeat some useful expressions on the CD-ROM.

Traditional Japanese games

Match the name of the traditional games and toys with their picture.

hana ichi monme

daruma otoshi

janken pon

origami

koma

fukuwarai

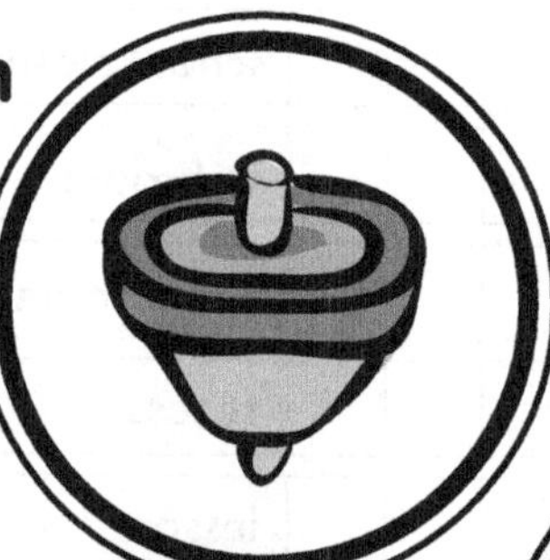

taketombo

kendama

Word Hint

あそびましょう。
a so bi ma sho u
Let's play.

かったー！
ka t ta a
We won!

まけた！
ma ke ta
We lost!

おめでとう！
o me de to u
Congratulations!

がんばって！
ga n ba t te
Go! Come on!

Traditional Toy Trail

Cross out the letters that appear more than twice and unjumble the remaining letters to reveal the hidden traditional toy.

S	B	I	G	U	K
J	K	E	J	P	O
R	P	N	O	G	K
H	T	G	B	K	A
A	N	P	B	P	N
E	B	D	J	E	M

じゃんけんポン
Janken Pon

This is Scissors, Paper, Rock with a twist. Try it out! Here are the words:

じゃんけんポン。
ja n ke n po n
Scissors, paper, rock.

あいこでしょう。
a i ko de sho u
It's a tie.

あっちむいてホイ！
a t chi mu i te ho i
Look that way!

Try it with a friend. You may even like to have a Janken Tournament in your class! Ask your teacher.

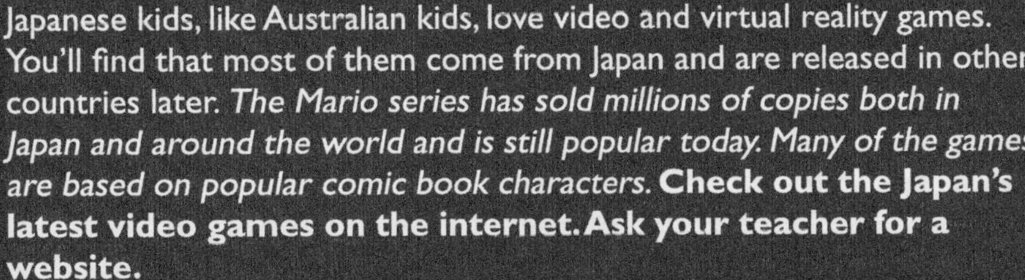

Japanese kids, like Australian kids, love video and virtual reality games. You'll find that most of them come from Japan and are released in other countries later. *The Mario series has sold millions of copies both in Japan and around the world and is still popular today. Many of the games are based on popular comic book characters.* **Check out the Japan's latest video games on the internet. Ask your teacher for a website.**

List the video games that you and your friends like playing now and google them to find out what year they came out in Japan. Then list the names of some of the new ones, which are popular in Japan now. Watch this space because they will be here soon too! This should be written in a mixture of fonts to make it look like kids talking.

What's hot here	Year	What's hot in Japan

あそびうた
Under the big chestnut tree

This is a well-known song with actions. Check it out on the CD-ROM .

おおきな くりの
o o ki na ku ri no

きのしたで
ki no shi ta de

あなたとわたし
a na ta to wa ta shi

なかよく
na ka yo ku

あそびましょう
a so bi ma sho u

おおきな くりの
o o ki na ku ri no

きのしたで
ki no shi ta de

The words mean:

Under the big chestnut tree

You and I will play nicely together

Under the big chestnut tree

はないちもんめ
The Hanaichimonme game

A two-team game, the object is to win extra players from the other team by winning a round of Scissors, Paper, Rock. Here are the words:

Team 1: かって うれしい はないちもんめ
ka t te u re shi i ha na i chi mo n me
We're so happy we won, hana ichi monme.

Team 2: まけて くやしい はないちもんめ
ma ke te ku ya shi i ha na i chi mo n me
We're so upset we lost, hana ichi monme.

Team 1: あのこ が ほしい
a no ko ga ho shi i
We want that kid.

Team 2: あのこ じゃわからん
a no ko ja wa ka ra n
We don't understand which kid you mean.

Team 1: そうだんしよう
so u da n shi yo u
Let's talk about it.

Team 2: そうだんしよう
so u da n shi yo u
Yes, let's.

Team 1: name of child chosen ちゃん が ほしい
cha n ga ho shi i
We want (name)-chan.

Team 2: name of child chosen ちゃん が ほしい
cha n ga ho shi i
We want (name)-chan.

Hey! I can:

- ☐ **Name some Japanese traditional toys and games**
- ☐ **Play some popular kids games**
- ☐ **Sing a song with actions**

⑬ たべものたのしい
Food Fun

Hey! Have you ever eaten Japanese food? You have, but only sushi? Not sure about the rest of the menu? Well here is your one stop guide to わしょく (*washoku*) – Japanese food.

すし
su shi

さしみ
sa shi mi

すきやき
su ki ya ki

てんぷら
te n pu ra

やきとり
ya ki to ri

しゃぶしゃぶ
sha bu sha bu

そば
so ba

おこのみやき
o ko no mi ya ki

うどん
u do n

The Big 3

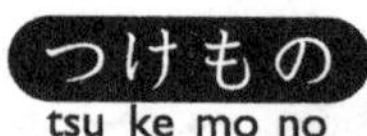

つけもの
tsu ke mo no

ごはん
go ha n

みそしる
mi so shi ru

おはしのつかいかた Using Chopsticks

Check out the CD-ROM for how to use chopsticks. Then play おはしリレー; chopsticks relay.

NEW STUFF きょうのポイント

なんですか。 na n de su ka	What is it?
______ です。 de su	It's ______.
おいしそうです。 o i shi so u de su	It looks nice.

Grab a friend

Take turns in pointing to each of the dishes.

- Ask what it is
- Answer what it is
- Say it looks nice

FOOD CROSS WORD

Use the clues to fill in the puzzle then find the mystery sentence.

CLUES:

1. A bowl of rice
2. Slices of raw fish and seafood
3. Thin buck wheat noodles in soup
4. Raw fish on mounds of vinegared rice
5. Grilled chicken on skewers
6. Thinly sliced beef and vegetables cooked in a sweet soy sauce, then dipped in raw egg
7. Savoury pancake containing cabbage and pork and seafood cooked on a hot plate
8. Pickled vegetables
9. Thick wheat noodles in a soup
10. Deep fried battered seafood and vegetables
11. Soup made from soy bean paste
12. Thinly sliced beef or pork cooked in a broth in the centre of the table

When you see all of this yummy **Japanese food you could say:**

____

SING

CD ROM Listen to the song on the CD-ROM, and then sing along!

ド・レ・ミ・ファ・そんぐ

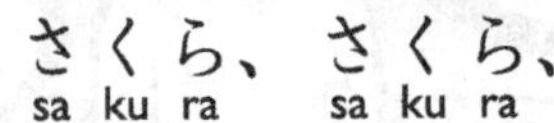

Sing the song to the tune of Sakura Sakura

さくら、さくら、
sa ku ra　sa ku ra

やきとり、てんぷら
ya ki to ri　te n pu ra

みそしる、さしみ
mi so shi ru　sa shi mi

ごはんとうめぼし
go ha n to u me bo shi

おちゃ、すし、おにぎり、
o cha　su shi　o ni gi ri

わさび、わさび
wa sa bi　wa sa bi

おこのみやき
o ko no mi ya ki

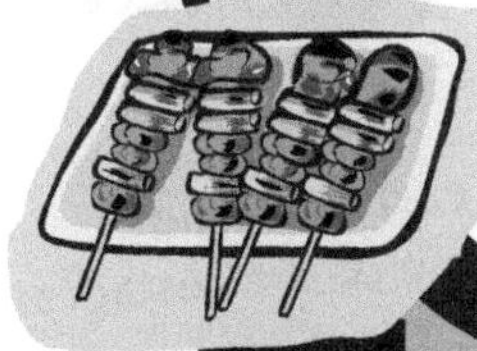

CD ROM Hey! I can:

- ☐ Recognize and describe 12 common Japan dishes
- ☐ Ask what something is and respond if someone asks me
- ☐ Say something looks delicious
- ☐ Sing a song about food

しゅくだい HOMEWORK:

Do a quick survey at home and find out which members of your family have eaten Japanese food and which dishes they have tried.

⑭レストランで
Eating Out

I think you are almost ready to eat out at a Japanese restaurant. But first you need to find out about a few of the customs and… learn a few manners!

天ぷら 天丼 親子丼 カツ丼 うな重 しょうが焼 焼き魚 煮魚

ごちそうさまでした。
go chi so u sa ma de shi ta

② ③ いらっしゃいませ！
i ra s sha i ma se

すみません、
su mi ma se n
メニューを
me nyu u o
ください。
ku da sa i

なにしますか。
na ni ni shi ma su ka

ありがとうございました。
a ri ga to u go za i ma shi ta

食堂

⑥ おしながき

⑤

おかんじょう
o ka n jo u
おねがいします。
o ne ga i shi ma su

④ 　　にします。
ni shi ma su

1. Many restaurants have a *noren* curtain in the doorway, which tells you the name of the restaurant or the type of food it serves.
2. When you enter the restaurant all waiters and chefs will call out welcome.
3. When you leave the restaurant all waiters and staff will call out thank you very much.
4. Water is usually free.
5. You will receive *waribashi*; wooden disposable chopsticks to eat with.
6. The menu often has photos of each item to help you.

Outside of the restaurant there will be a glass cabinet with plastic models of most of the dishes on the menu even the drinks, so you can check out the menu and the prices before you go in.

If the restaurant has a red lantern out the front it means that it is not too expensive.

Some restaurants have private rooms for large groups which have tatami on the floor. In these, you will need to take off your shoes and sit on a cushion on the floor at a low table.

NEW STUFF きょうのポイント

There are a few expressions that are very important when you are having a meal in Japan.

いただきます。 i ta da ki ma su	おいしいです。 o i shi i de su	これはちょっと…… ko re wa cho t to
ごちそうさまでした。 go chi so u sa ma de shi ta	とてもおいしいです。 to te mo o i shi i de su	もうけっこうです。 mo u ke k ko u de su

Fill in the blanks with an appropriate expression from the list.

Before you start to eat you should always say ________ ______________ with a little bow of your head. As you eat you can pick up your rice bowl and raise it to your mouth as you take food from your different plates. If you take something from a dish in the middle of the table, which is for everyone, you should turn your chopsticks around and pick it up with the clean end of your chopsticks and put it on your plate. Usually, someone will ask you how you like the meal. You can say ____________ __________ or, if you really like it you can say ______________________. You should NEVER say it's horrible, even if it is! But you can say ______________________. When you have had enough to eat you can say ______________________. At the end of the meal you should say ______________________ with another little bow.

CD ROM Eating Right

Check out the CD for some eating etiquette.

しゅくだい HOMEWORK:

Jump onto the internet or into the phone book and find out the names of some Japanese restaurants in your area. You may even be able to view their menus.

CD ROM Hey! I can:

- ☐ Order food in a restaurant in Japanese
- ☐ Ask for a menu or the bill
- ☐ Talk about kinds of restaurants in Japan
- ☐ Talk about customs in restaurants
- ☐ Talk about eating etiquette

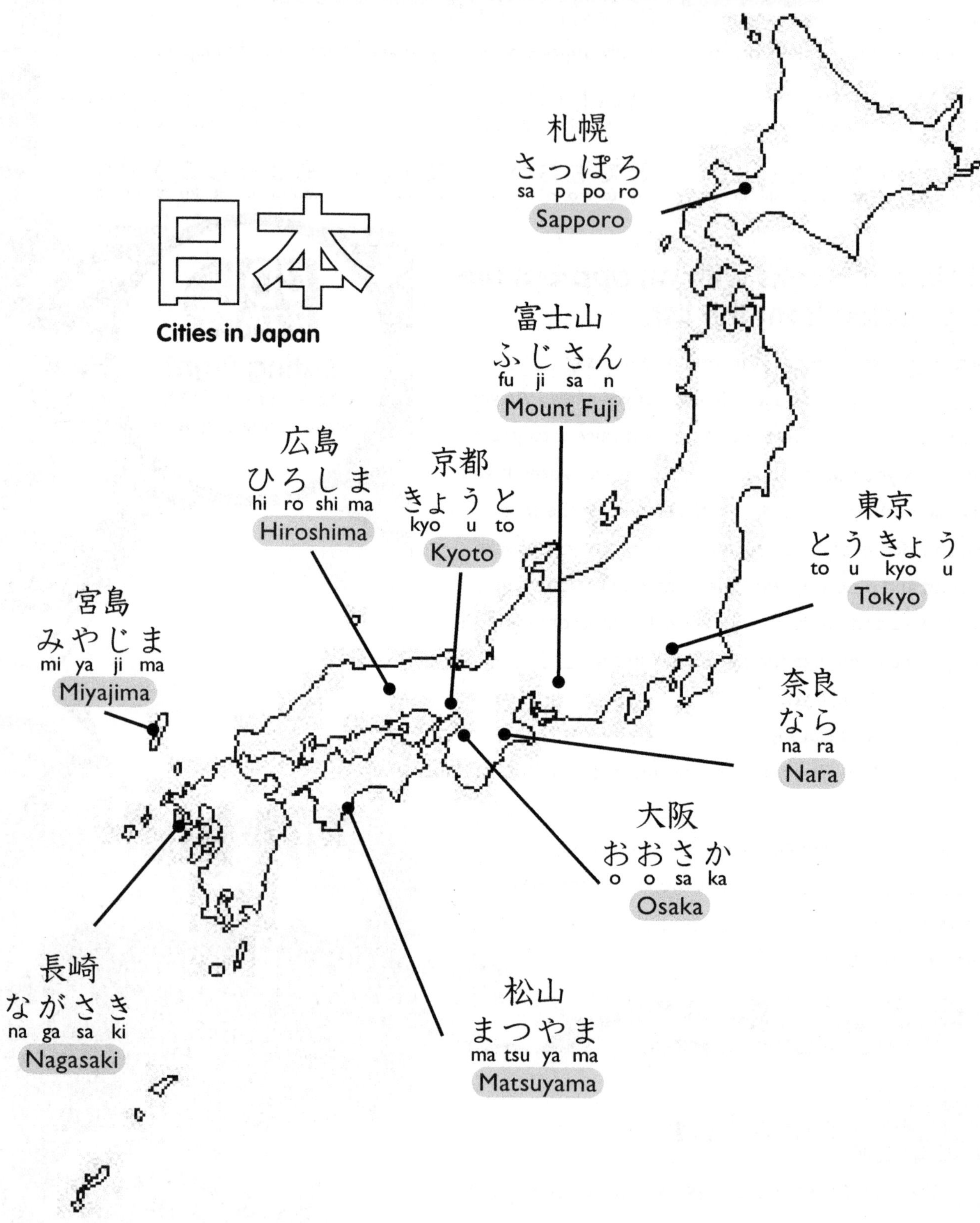
日本
Cities in Japan
札幌
さっぽろ
sa p po ro
Sapporo
富士山
ふじさん
fu ji sa n
Mount Fuji
広島
ひろしま
hi ro shi ma
Hiroshima
京都
きょうと
kyo u to
Kyoto
東京
とうきょう
to u kyo u
Tokyo
宮島
みやじま
mi ya ji ma
Miyajima
奈良
なら
na ra
Nara
大阪
おおさか
o o sa ka
Osaka
長崎
ながさき
na ga sa ki
Nagasaki
松山
まつやま
ma tsu ya ma
Matsuyama